Lifelong Frenemies

Lifelong Frenemies

A Guide to Transitioning from Perfection to Civility and Staying Friendly with your Co-Parent

JACQUELINE EPSTEIN

J. Kenkade
PUBLISHING®

Little Rock, Arkansas

Lifelong Frenemies
Copyright © 2017 by Jacqueline Epstein

All rights reserved. No part of this book may be photocopied, reproduced, distributed, uploaded, or transmitted in any form or by any means, or stored in a database or retrieval system, without the prior written permission of the publisher.

J. Kenkade Publishing
6104 Forbing Rd
Little Rock, AR 72209
www.jkenkade.com
Facebook.com/JKenkade
J. Kenkade Publishing is a registered trademark.

PrintedintheUnitedStatesofAmerica
ISBN 978-1-944486-95-2

This book recounts actual events in the life of Jacqueline Epstein according to the author's recollection and perspective. Some of the identifying details may have been changed to respect the privacy of those involved. The views expressed in this book are those of the author and do not necessarily reflect the views of Publisher.

Disclaimer: Nothing contained in this book should be construed as legal advice. This work is intended for a general audience and does not create an attorney-client relationship.

*This book is dedicated to my daughters,
Avivah and Sephorah, you make my life a
beautiful place to be.*

Table of Contents

Foreword		11
Chapter 1	Seafood on the Countertop	21
Chapter 2	Free as a Bird	31
Chapter 3	Control Freak	39
Chapter 4	Peace Out	49
Chapter 5	Let It Be	57
Chapter 6	Frenemy Synergy	63
Chapter 7	The Dog Ate My Homework	71
Chapter 8	Other Mothering/Bother Fathering	79
Chapter 9	Paper Chasing	93
Chapter 10	Burnt Pancakes	103
Chapter 11	Your House Sucks	111
Chapter 12	Kindergarten Basics	115
About the Author		123
Appendix		125
References		129

Foreword by my Frenemy, Jeremy Epstein

It may at first seem odd that Jacqueline's former husband would write the foreword to her book. But, that really is the point of this book. Co-parenting takes two. We remain co-parents to two amazingly beautiful daughters, and even... dare I say, we remain friends. Co-parenting is about something bigger than the issues that ended the marriage. It's about the fact that you and your ex are the only parents your children will ever have, and that makes you and your ex family no matter what. And that's why I am writing the foreword to my ex-wife's primer on divorce and custody. We are divorced, but we are still family and always will be. And like it or not, you will remain family with your ex too. So, buckle up and enjoy the rollercoaster ride. It's bumpy, but it's yours. I cannot explain the countless times that friends and colleagues tell Jacqueline and me that it is so strange how well we get along considering we are divorced. We can work well together and can be very amicable for short periods of time. Jacqueline refers to us as "seafood on the counter." She is right. We are good for as long as 3 hours. No more. Something happens at the 3-hour mark. For 3 hours, we can attend a joint party together. We can work together in court. We can be together for 3 hours without the issues of the past rearing their ugly heads. But more than 3 hours… no. As a father, I believe strongly in getting along with your child's other parent.

I believe in showing your children that you are family and that family does for family. Family spends time with family, and Jacqueline and I show our kids that for as long as humanly possible—which for us is 3 hours. Being a parent is hard. Time to reflect and rejuvenate is necessary. It helps you be a better parent and a better co-parent since you have time to clear your head and be yourself. I find that it is very important to have a clear schedule for custody so that you can plan your kid-free time while still knowing that your children are safe and being cared for. That kid-free time should be both restorative and, honestly…fun.

Having adult friendships is very important for a single parent. You should be able to delineate "parent-time" and "me-time," and doing this will help you be better both ways. I like to go to the movies. It clears my head. I also like to travel. This makes me feel like I can be myself—not just the kids' dad.

Lifelong Frenemies

Jacqueline likes to spend time with friends, and she also likes to travel. While our methods are different, the result is the same. We are better co-parents when we get the necessary time to be ourselves. Do not neglect yourself in this process. This is a "work hard, play hard" game.

Be the best parent you can be when it's time to be a parent.

Be your best self you can be when it's time to let the other parent do their own parenting.

That last sentence there about the other party's "own parenting," is important. You will become very familiar with words like "domiciliary parent" (or "managing conservator" in some states). On the surface, this means the person that is charged with making the ultimate decisions regarding the children's health, education and general welfare. But that's not really the end of the story, is it? Yes, there are two parents. There will always be two people who are co-parenting. Sometimes each parent's co-parenting involves significant input from others.

However, for the two parents, the rules should be the same. The two co-parents understand their children better than anyone else, and they should be the ones making the final decisions when it involves the children. In our situation, Jacqueline is the "domiciliary parent." But we work together to make the best decisions for our children. Our kids go to schools we discussed and looked at together. Camp, though it was a hard decision, was one we came to as a co-parenting team.

But when it comes to the style with which we parent the kids on our own time, we are **very** different. Jacqueline believes in a more hands-off approach that focuses on the simple things in life (like letting the kids hang out at home and have simple food and entertainment options). I believe in giving the kids lots of new experiences (like eating in restaurants and finding entertainment outside the house). We **do not** always agree on these differences in how we parent. But, at the end of the day, and for the most part, we allow the other to parent in their own style, and I think the kids are better off for having both types of parenting. This leads to well-rounded children who enjoy something special about each parent. As long as you are discussing important issues, and as long as you choose your battles, you can have an amicable parenting scenario overall.

Allowing each co-parent to parent in their own way does not mean that you and your co-parent cannot be on the same page with the big things. And sometimes, the big things don't seem like *big* things. A good example is your children's diet. A child will generally try to eat the worst possible things available to them. My kids particularly enjoy chocolate and sweets. But you cannot let them rule the world of their diet because it will become a big issue. So, what do you do? Well, Jacqueline and I fought a bit about it, but after deliberation, we decided together that the kids should eat better. And while I would still take them out to eat at restaurants, and she would still give them basic options at home, as co-parents, we decided that there would be certain foods that we would both steer the kids toward and certain foods we would both adamantly refuse to allow. Thus, we were able to harmonize the parenting styles to fit the need—not change the style overall.

Both Jacqueline and I focus our practices on issues involving family law, and our experiences in court with custody and visitation have helped shape how we handle custody and visitation with our own children. Many times, parents in the heat of a custody battle make demands that they, and they alone, shall have most of the children's time allotted to them. And it makes for great fireworks in and out of the courtroom! But it does not make happy co-parents and happy children. As co-parents, you should both think about how custody is going to shape your daily lives.

How will custody affect your ability to work? Who will watch the kids when you work? Will you be able to have the children for that many school breaks or for that long? When will you get your necessary "me-time?" These are things that we *never* think about in the heat of the battle! But these are the most important things to consider. For example, our children seem to have a week-long break almost every month. We did not even consider that when deciding our custody schedule. But now, we work together to ensure everyone can work as needed. We have worked together to change how we do holidays so that the way our separate lives really work can work with the kid's holiday schedules. Our custody agreement said that we alternate Christmas and New Year's, whereas practicality dictated that Christmas will always be with Jacqueline's family because they celebrate Christmas and my family does not. But now the kids always look forward to New Year's celebrations with Dad's family like clockwork. And we help each other with school drop-off if the other has court, and we work together to make sure each can attend important events.

In this book, this working relationship is referred to as "frenemy synergy," and that could not be more correct. You will both love and hate each other at various times, but you will always need to work together! Another thing that helps keep the peace: exchanges that run with school and/or camp drop-offs and pick-ups. A few major child meltdowns at the house will tell you this is a good idea. Personally, I find that that co-parents should be just that—co-parents. As in two parents. But what happens when in-laws and new partners decide they know better? They don't; not about your kids. Go with your own gut.

Get that "frenemy synergy" going!

Every discussion about child custody inevitably

Lifelong Frenemies

involves a discussion about child support. Chances are if you are reading this book, child support is an issue in your future. Child support is not meant to cover all of the child's expenses. It is not meant to support the parent or relieve the other parent of their financial obligations. It is, simply put, help. Child support helps ensure that the children have a roof over their heads, lights on, transportation, food and clothing. It is not a substitute for the financial responsibilities of parenting. And the co-parents should help each other.

Children are expensive. Schools are expensive. Before- and after-school care is expensive. Camps are expensive. Clothes and entertainment are expensive. Did I mention, *children are expensive*?! Keeping that in mind, just because you no longer live together doesn't mean that children become less expensive. So, what can you do? Work together to ensure the children get their financial needs met. For those who pay child support, that means you need to keep in mind that it might not be just your court-ordered monthly amount. It might be more, and your parent-mode should kick in and go, "It's for my kids! I won't fight about it!"

My suggestion: Keep records, and don't make cash payments. For those who receive child support, make every dollar you get to help support the kids count. Don't waste the money; Make sure it gives your kids the leg-up they need. So, how do you keep expenses down? My suggestion, talk about the expenses and decide what works for everyone. No one can afford to ignore those conversations. It's about the kids, folks!

At this point, you're probably getting a clear picture that I believe in working together with your ex to co-parent your kids. And you are right because the kids need you, not your fighting. I also know that it must be very nice for someone to sit here and write a foreword that says, *"Can't we all just get along?"* and I know how unrealistic that will seem. In the beginning, it may very well be unrealistic. But it doesn't have to be a dirty dog fight for 18 years. Your kids will remember how each co-parent was long after they "age out of the system." So, do your best to make good examples for your children, and do what you can to make it amicable.

There is no shame in using dispute resolution options such as mediation to help you negotiate through the hard parts. No one wins, especially not the children when the court has to decide in a few hours how your life will be lived. And while that's available, it's not in the best interest of the children. So, if you really can't work through the issues, go get some help! Negotiation will nearly always be beneficial to the end result, even if you need a mediator to help you be in the same room as each other. And your kids won't notice it was this hard. They will just be able to bask in the awesomeness of their parents working together for their benefit.

So, there you go: Quick thoughts from someone

Lifelong Frenemies

who both lives these guidelines and works through these types of issues for others for a living. Jacqueline has worked hard to give you the nitty-gritty of each issue and to help you really be better co-parents. But I hope that I have given you some food for thought. You really can raise amazing kids together while not being a couple. And I have all the confidence in the world that you can do it! We did!
-Jeremy Epstein

1

SEAFOOD ON THE COUNTERTOP
Amicability with your Ex

Being a divorced divorce attorney who is amicable with my ex, I hear from people all the time, "How do you do it? How do you stay friends with your ex-husband?" I always answer the same thing: "Our relationship is like 'seafood on a counter top.' After an hour and a half, it goes bad and needs to be put away. No matter how much it seems like it will not spoil, it is going to head that direction and needs some fresh air, before everyone regrets it." In my mind, an hour and a half is the timeframe that I can typically hang out in the same place with my ex without mentally preparing to hold back my opinions and thoughts on almost everything. Despite my profession, which requires me to argue on a regular basis, I tend to be conflict averse in my personal life. Call it a casualty of my job, but I'm exhausted by the time my professional hat comes off and the last thing I want to do is argue my own custody issues or relationship problems. I have found that this level of aversion to arguing in my personal life has served well in my ability to co-parent. The goal has always been to avoid conflict with my ex. The task of conflict avoidance is a difficult one. There are days where both my ex and I are feeling insecure about life in general and we naturally rehash the whole "I was right, you were wrong about our breakup" discussion, seeking personal validation even though we both know that we are better as friends. The transition from "wronged partner" and "right partner" to just two regular people who can't live together is a challenging one.

When Jeremy and I split, we were not friendly with each other.

As he moved his things out of our former home, we shouted at each other so much that the movers went on break to avoid listening to it.

To this day, I still want him to slip on a banana peel so I can laugh hysterically, and he has no reservations whatsoever about telling me that I'm stubborn and opinionated. But when it comes down to it, I don't want harm to come to him because I spent almost a decade of my life planning and building a future with him as my teammate, and

Lifelong Frenemies

we both still benefit from the hard work we started as young people. We have two amazing daughters, and both of us enriched one another's careers. Jeremy learned how to save money from the things I learned growing up in a less affluent background than him, and I learned about entrepreneurship from his experience growing up in a family that owned businesses for generations. All in all, after a decade, people influence one another's lives for the better and for the worse. I still care very much for his father and sister, and he still talks to my mom and my sister. Because family is family and despite the fact that sometimes the sound of his voice makes me want to catch the first plane to a remote location with no cellphone reception, I know that we have to make our friendship work for our kids. I am not advocating that all former couples can remain friends. In my line of work, I see cases where there has been physical abuse and mental abuse that is so traumatic that neither partner can overcome the interpersonal problems that exist. In those cases, I generally recommend the parents seek the help of a mental health professional.

In order to create a healthy co-parenting environment, insecurity cannot be an overriding factor.

In my opinion, in order to create a healthy co-parenting environment, insecurity cannot be an overriding factor.

Both an abuser and victim tend to have self-esteem issues that create a lasting effect on their ability to parent their children, much less create a healthy relationship with their co-parent. In a lot of circumstances, the abuse takes another form after the breakup. However, in cases where both parties feel they can speak up for themselves without the fear of substantial harm, co-parenting amicably is ideal for the children and can benefit both parties.

If you are reading this book, then you or those involved in your case believe that there is a possibility of reaching a healthy relationship in an extended family setting.

There *will* be issues and arguments!

If you had a perfect relationship with your ex, then you would still be living together.

The goal has to transition from potential reconciliation and perfection, to recognizing that the personalities involved in the former relationship are incompatible but unique and beneficial to the children. I leave the house and go to public places. Sometimes I interact with people who I find rude, insensitive and poorly mannered. However, I do not have an investment in the outcome of their lives, so it does not bother me tremendously that they have behaved negatively in my presence. I interact with people who have different religious, political and moral viewpoints than my own. Very seldom do these interactions result in a heated, verbal exchange.

During these unpleasant or unfamiliar interactions, I am aware of two things:
1. I am not responsible for agreeing with or changing this person's point of view or behavior.
2. I can leave if I am truly uncomfortable.

Now that you have ended your romantic relationship, this is the situation you are in with your ex. Make no mistake, you are not responsible for your ex's behavior and you are free to leave at any time. Today, I had one of those arguments with my ex where all the stops were pulled out. With both my ex and I being family law attorneys, this can get ugly.

For every argument we made, we were flinging case law around like confetti and dropping litigation threats like it was hot!

It got petty fast!

So, we walked away and came back 20 minutes later. We had an agreement within a half-hour. Again, I think our professional knowledge helps us get through the petty portion of the argument more quickly, *but it is truly the walking away that allows us both to reevaluate the desire to be right at all costs; because more likely than not, that cost is born by our children.* When heated disputes arise (which they inevitably will), I recommend to my clients that they step away and transition the discussion to text messages or emails. It seems that when someone has to take the time to write out their statements, they are more likely to put thought into the wording and are less likely to say things they don't mean. I use this method personally. If I am on a telephone call with my ex and we start to argue, I end the call and wait 10 minutes or so before texting my points in an effort to resolve the dispute. I have found that most times, this ends with my ex and me sending each other "hug" emojis and ending the argument.

It is very difficult to speak cautiously when you are emotional, and it is even more difficult to listen effectively. Written communication helps to resolve those problems. Also, there are days where my ex and I will attend parties with mutual friends or have lunch to discuss the children or cases we still have together from what remains of our law firm. Since we work in the same field, we have several occasions where we are in the same place aside from our obligations to functions for our children. Many times, we are not in good relations during these functions. It is important that both parents realize that there are people more important than your ex attending these events, your kids, or in my case, kids, friends, clients, judges… the list goes on. No one, especially your children, wants to witness a post-breakup rehash of every infraction the other person committed during the relationship. No one thinks you are right and the other person is wrong.

Lifelong Frenemies

You are both wrong because this is not the time for that discussion!

It is important that both parties enter those scenarios with full acceptance that:
1. The other parent is present.
2. The issues you both have with each other will not be resolved at THIS event.
3. You are both there for a purpose other than each other, and that purpose is more important than anything else.

There are even circumstances that could exacerbate the hostility level, such as the presence of former in-laws or new dating partners. Again, the children are the priority in this scenario and it is important as a good parent that you keep the eye on the ball of parenting in that situation.

Keep in mind, you can leave at any time.

You aren't together anymore, so you have no obligation to make small talk or win anyone over.

You can walk away from the ex, the new dating partner or the former in-law. You can excuse yourself to the restroom or the parking lot.

When you step away to regain perspective, you can pursue this goal more effectively.

Before, when you were together, your ex's opinion and the opinion of his loved ones mattered tremendously because you were trying to cultivate those relationships. Now, those relationships have changed, and civility is the only requirement.

Sometimes, my ex and I will get along well. We might have lunch and discuss a variety of things we have obligations to complete related to work and the children. Things seem to be going pretty well, like we are true friends. Keep in mind that despite the illusion that *all* is well, old issues will inevitably creep into the conversation if you continue to extend your time together. The competitive determination of which one of us is succeeding at life and which one of us is the bad guy always lingers in the background. **I call this "Frenemy Mode."** We both know neither one of us wants the other to fail for the children's sake, but we still seek the vindication of feeling like the better person. The reality is the marriage didn't work; neither of us were the better person. We just weren't the right people. We are *lifelong frenemies*. We will support each other for the betterment of our children to the extent that the other does not benefit more than ourselves. And that is ok.

This is where my "seafood on the countertop" rule comes in to play. My experience is that good things come to an end with exes. It is better to end the conversation or meeting on a positive note where the next conversation or meeting can begin productively than to extend this situation and take the chance of a turn for the worst. Your mutual goals have changed, and it is easy to forget that the level of investment in the relationship is not the same.

Lifelong Frenemies

My ex and I have about an hour and a half on an average day, without advanced planning, before things go sour. This took a period of trial and error to determine. At first, we couldn't be in the same room at all. After a few months, we could go thirty minutes. It is now a year and a half since our split, and we are good for an hour and a half. Every family has a different window of time, and yours is for you to determine. I do not

After an hour or so, I know it's time to wrap things up before they spoil, just like seafood on a countertop.

run a timer, but after an hour or so, I know it's time to wrap things up before they spoil, just like seafood on a countertop. We still plan longer events with our kids periodically. Our oldest daughter is going to sleepaway camp next week 200 miles away from our hometown, and we have decided to drive her there together, three hours each way in the car. We have discussed in advance that an argument is likely and resolved that we will not argue on the road trip.

If we notice an argument brewing, we plan to stop and get out of the car for a while.

It is important that you don't forget the reasons why your partnership did not work, but recognize that those issues weren't able to be resolved. At some point, you fought to maintain the relationship and were afraid of being alone or starting over with someone new, but the issues between you and your ex were too great to overcome. This was evident when you split. Otherwise, you would still be together, and you aren't. *Rehashing those issues will only further sever the remains of your friendship.* Therefore, it is important that you recognize that at the end of it all, you can still be happy with your children, have a healthy romantic life and keep a good lifelong frenemy who truly doesn't want to see you fail.

FREE AS A BIRD
Valuing Your Kid-Free Time

The first few months after my separation and custody agreement with Jeremy, I felt extremely lonely and empty during the times he had visitation with the kids. I found myself binge watching more Netflix than I was proud to admit. I remembered all the things I wanted to do when I was married. I wanted to have a truly organized home, learn Krav Maga, get back into sailing (which I hadn't had time to do since college), and perfect my Greek conversation skills. But when we separated and the reality of having a quiet home several nights per month came to fruition, I was lost. It took me at least a month before I was comfortable enough to begin the organization projects I had in mind. So, the first extended period that the kids were gone was the second half of winter break during the week of New Years. I called in reinforcements: My mom, dad and sister came to my house and helped me strategize, repaint walls and rearrange furniture. I organized closets and went through old mail. I was on a mission to clean. During this time, I had very little social interaction. Most of my friends were married with children.

My married friends, for the most part, didn't want to get involved in hanging out with Jeremy and me separately because they feared that our breakup was extraordinarily hostile, and they understandably wanted to stay neutral.

So, I relied heavily on my family to fill that void.

Next, I bought an old sailboat from a kid who left for college and couldn't bring it along. It needed paint and interior work, so I spent my kid-free weekends refinishing the boat.

But I still found myself exceedingly lonely.

I had decided not to date for a while, and I had few friends who were kid-free who had the ability to socialize at will.

I decided to gain a policy of accepting every single invitation I received. I was invited to birthday parties for kids and adults, high school reunions, and professional networking events. I attended everything I could when my kids were gone. I also supplemented the time by signing up for every class and seminar I could find. I went night sailing on a boat with strangers. I decided I wanted a social life, so I created one. Facebook, Meetup and Eventbrite were my primary resources for meeting people and getting out of my house. I decided that staying home and reorganizing the already-organized closets eventually became negative behavior. I felt more out of sorts as I tried to create the gold standard of *clean* and *organized*. I needed people and lots of them.

I have an exceptionally social friend who attended the same high school as me. She volunteers for charities, organizes mixers and even hosts 5k races. She began inviting me to different events—her birthday party, a twerk class at the Jewish Community Center and a music festival. As antisocial as I was feeling at the time, I forced myself to get dressed and go participate.

Before I knew it, I was 10 friends deep on a cruise and was parasailing my way over the Mexican Riviera.

I also planned to travel alone.

It is amazing how people react when you answer the question "How are you doing?" with "Great actually, I am going to Las Vegas next month."

One of my very best friends, who was only an acquaintance at the time, asked to join me on the trip, and we have been inseparable ever since. By choosing to join things and really experience the things I couldn't do while my children were with me, I created a great social circle of supportive friends. I have a policy when it comes to my kid-free time. I refuse to do anything that my children would be unhappy that I did without them. Sometimes I eat pizza, but I am referring to the big stuff. I was in Los Angeles recently with someone I was dating and the suggestion was made that we spend the day at Disneyland. That was a firm "N.O." for me! I choose to keep my activities with the children related to family things they are interested in, and I keep those things exclusive to my time with them. This ensures they have the best experiences when they are with me and also that they feel nothing is lost during their visitation time with their dad. The time when I do not have my children, I spend working around my house, hanging out with my kid-free friends, dating and doing adult-only activities. This is the time to stroll through an art gallery, learn a foreign language or go attend that yoga class. The kids won't care because they have no interest, and you probably can't participate with the children present anyhow.

I have a policy when it comes to my kid-free time. I refuse to do anything that my children would be unhappy that I did without them.

I also like to do my grocery shopping, errand running and any work I took home from the office at that time. I found a two-part benefit to handling the errands when the kids are with their dad. First, I don't get badgered to buy Oreos and Playdough at the register (and I have saved a small fortune) and second, I don't spend the time I do have with my kids running them all over town. We spend that time at home, enjoying each other's company.

I have received criticism, particularly from my married friends with kids, that I have a great social life and it isn't fair. Alternatively, I have heard that I seem like a "lot of fun," usually accompanied with a negative and judgmental tone. Even my lifelong frenemy seems jealous and judgmental when I have plans during my kid-free time. However, I have firmly cemented in my mind that I am comfortable with my time budgeting for several reasons.

It is very important to remember that before, when you were married, someone was there and they most likely helped in some way. They may have taken out the trash or helped earn the money or even watched the children periodically, so you could do those things.

Now, it's just *you*.

My married friends with kids do not understand that I am putting in 100% of the work more than 50% of the time, and that is the equivalent to the same or more effort toward child-rearing obligations that existed during my married life. Additionally, there is the actualization that adult interaction is now at a deficit compared to what it was during your married life. As I have stated before, I am cautious about integrating my dating partners into my children's lives so that "free time" without the kids is in many cases the only time I have to meet people. When I am not dating, I spend that time with friends, enjoying the activities that I once enjoyed before I had children and participating in community activities and organizations to which I belonged while I was married. *No matter how much I love my children, they will never understand my tough day at work like another adult, and they shouldn't.* I approach my off-visitation custody time as an opportunity to recharge for when the children return because it is hard! It is hard to be the only adult at the time when they ask their questions, the only adult doing the epic laundry, the only adult making the lunches and doing the homework.

When they leave my home to go to their dad's house, I unapologetically relax, socialize and join the adult world because Monday at school pick-up until next weekend, the spotlight is on me and me alone.

I find that having time away from the kids also gives me the time to reevaluate my parenting pitfalls. I have an opportunity to plan my next goals and strategies for better parenting my kids. Right now, aside from writing this book, I have used my summer custody switch to clean out the kids closets and shuffle clothing sizes, plan an after-school schedule, and decide which extracurricular activities I want to enroll the kids in during the school year. I've had a chance to think without being interrupted by requests and responsibilities related to the kids' immediate needs. I highly recommend that you use your kid-free time to prepare for the time when you will have custody again. Set goals. Reevaluate the household routine. When the kids return from their co-parent visitation, you will be ready to give parenting your undivided and well-strategized attention. Ultimately, the kids will benefit.

CONTROL FREAK
Keeping Parental Control through Amicability

One of the most valuable things I have maintained through staying amicable with my ex-husband is my parental authority. My friendship with Jeremy, albeit rocky at times, has allowed me to keep my parenting style relatively uninterrupted. My daughters are extremely spirited, and Jeremy and I were both raised in very different environments. My parents took a less structured approach to parenting whereas Jeremy's parents were extremely involved in helping him make his decisions. Both of us clash at times because of our upbringings. Jeremy believes that he should take a significant role in directing the children and structuring their choices to ensure those choices and behaviors are successful. I believe in a trial-

and-error learning approach. I prefer to advise the children on the benefits and consequences of their choices and let them decide based on their own deduction. I began this parenting approach early in their lives. I distinctly remember telling my two-year-old that jumping on the sofa was a bad idea and that although it was fun, she could fall and hurt herself. Sure enough, she fell moments after I rendered my advisory opinion on sofa jumping. I picked her up from the floor, kissed her boo-boo and reiterated to her the learning experience knowing that in the future she would make her decisions independently and more carefully.

Amicability facilitates discussions that the court cannot order in a judgment.

In the same scenario, Jeremy's approach would be to tell her to stop jumping on the sofa or she would proceed to a time out.

While, in my opinion, this is effective to prevent this particular mistake, it does not teach her how to prevent ongoing mistakes and effectively make decisions independently. This is a perspective on which he and I strongly disagree. I am fully committed to creating independent thinkers, whether or not their decisions result in negative consequences and whether or not I have to replace my sofa. Jeremy is mistake-preventative and focuses on avoiding the negative consequences.

Since Jeremy and I are amicable, we discuss these things. There is no court order requiring us to discuss parenting style and how it will affect our children as adults. We choose to discuss these things because we both diligently work toward our common goal to raise well-adjusted and successful adults. Amicability facilitates discussions that the court cannot order in a judgment. The type of conversations about the children that occurs when parents are married should continue after the separation. Court orders in Louisiana often require that the co-parents confer about medical, religious, educational and extracurricular activities, but not about giving the children advice, discipline and structure. These issues are equally important in raising well-adjusted successful adults. However, the court system cannot regulate the parenting style unless it becomes abusive to the child. Amicability allows the co-parents to raise the children effectively beyond the issues specified in the court judgment.

Parenting is more challenging now than at any time in history.

Outside influences are available at children's fingertips with the abundant access to technology. That doesn't even include the interactions your children have with classmates, friends and other adults. Combating negative influences is a huge feat even in two-parent households. By creating an open line of communication through amicable relationships with your co-parent, you increase the family's ability to parent in a manner that benefits your children tremendously.

One less than enjoyable evening, Jeremy had the children, and I was at dinner with friends when my older daughter decided to throw a massive hissy fit at bedtime.

Jeremy was frustrated and desperate. He called me to intervene.

I left dinner and went to his house. With both of us there, Jeremy was able to put our younger daughter, who was exhausted and up way past her bedtime, to sleep while I managed the hissy fit situation. The next morning, I received a phone call from my refreshed and more reasonable daughter, who apologized for her behavior. Crisis averted through amicable co-parenting, and I anticipate many more situations like this will occur in the future.

My children are four and eight years old. At present, bedtime is one of the biggest obstacles to parenting. But I envision a time where friends, dating partners, academics and peer pressure present greater challenges. I hope that through amicable co-parenting, I am able to work with Jeremy to successfully surpass the inevitable challenges that will arise over the next fourteen years or more. I strongly believe fear of failure drives much of our amicability. Neither of us want to fail at parenting,

Lifelong Frenemies

and the odds are better if we work as a team.

Much like a team, however, there are challenges. We already discussed disputes on methods of parenting, but in addition, there are power struggles. The "I am the better parent" debate rages on as we struggle to determine who should be entitled to the team recognition. I am guilty of this. My daughter tested extremely well on her state standardized tests last year. I have custody of the kids four school nights per week, so I bragged on Facebook about the amazing job I must be doing. *Not my best co-parenting moment.*

Jeremy has a habit of sharing every outing he and the children take on Facebook. Every zoo visit, every ice cream cone, every festival… right there on Facebook. It is frustrating.

The competition for the "Best Parent" label is fierce! At the end of the day, neither of us can do the quality of job we are doing without help from the other and every so often, we say that to each other. Despite our best parent trophy epic throwdown, the reality is we both care how it all turns out, and overall, it is the kids who win.

The kids win our effort and our concern that we aren't as adequate as parents as we were before the divorce. It is the concern that they will suffer from our mistakes that drives us to remain frenemies, working as a team but seeking the recognition that our individual effort was the winning factor.

Nonetheless, like a team, we are constantly competing with one another for the parenting trophy and improving the team as we improve ourselves. As long as the competition remains healthy, I think it benefits the kids. I am a proponent of channeling all my aggravation with my ex into being the best parent because directing that frenemy energy toward improving things for the kids is productive and beneficial to us all.

Amicability allows me to voice my opinion more frequently than if my ex and I didn't get along well.

So, I say, "Haha, I'm better than you… at reading stories and making flash cards and attending swim lessons!"

And even though it is annoying, I couldn't care less if he says, "No, I'm better than you… at going to the zoo and traveling with our kids and bringing them to religious services."

We can argue for hours, and I put up a good fight, but I walk away every single time smiling because we are parenting well. Amicability allows me to voice my opinion more frequently than if my ex and I didn't get along well. I can call him and tell him that bedtime in my house moved back 15 minutes because the kids seemed difficult to awaken in the morning and I would like him to keep the bedtime consistent. Since he and I get along pretty well, he listens to my rationale and implements the bedtime. Likewise, he calls me to tell me that my older daughter now likes to eat broccoli and that I should buy some since she despised it before eating it at school that day.

As an attorney, I can conclusively say that the court system does not address bedtimes and vegetable choices. Not to mention, the attorneys' fees associated with disputing these types of things would likely be astronomical. Nonetheless, these issues are important in raising children. Amicability is the reason that bedtimes aren't inconsistent, and the children eat as much broccoli as they want in our households. That stability is beneficial to the children.

Sometimes, the voice co-parents maintain through amicability must be used for issues that are more controversial. Prior to my divorce, my younger daughter attended preschool at the same preschool I attended as a child. When Jeremy moved out of our home, he moved into an apartment in a different part of town and it was difficult for him to arrange transportation to and from the preschool on his visitation days. He wanted to change the preschool. I was firmly against the idea, but because he and I were amicable and I had an interest in remaining amicable, I toured the preschool closer to his apartment. I was very pleased with the preschool, and we chose to let our daughter switch schools.

My cooperation with the preschool change was not required. In Louisiana, the domiciliary parent makes the decisions about education, religious, medical and extracurricular activities subject to the non-domiciliary parent's right to object. I am the domiciliary parent, so I could have refused. I would have probably won if the issue went to court since our daughter already attended the preschool of my choosing and the courts strive to provide consistency for the children. I chose to tour the new school because despite the right I had to refuse, I believe that my ex would not consider making such a drastic change unless he felt that some benefit would come to our daughter as a result.

I recognized that as her father, he would not seek to make a change that was not in her best interest.

The new school was surprisingly advanced by comparison to the preschool I had attended as a child. By the end of the tour, it did not matter to me if the motivation for the change was Jeremy's convenience or enhanced academic preparation. I agreed with the switch.

If communication was limited because Jeremy and I lacked amicability, I would have asserted my right to make the educational decision as domiciliary parent, *and my daughter wouldn't have received the benefit of the new school.* I recognized that as her father, Jeremy would not seek to make a change that was not in her best interest. So, I attended the school tour. There was no need to assert my dominant legal status or get into a heated exchange.

Lifelong Frenemies

The goal of providing maximum benefit to our children is shared, and though we may not always agree on the methods used to attain that goal, we are able to converse about the methods in a meaningful way because we are amicable.

Peace Out
Handling Suggestions of Reconciliation in an Amicable(ish) Split

I abhor that people assume that since my ex and I are amicable, we will eventually reconcile. Yesterday, this happened to me twice. "Well, look at the happy couple!" and "You two are so cute." These comments both came separately from two female family law attorney friends who know very well that I am divorced. I was less than thrilled. Both of these ladies know that amicability is a requirement as they both practice law in the family courts regularly. Yet, the concept that two divorced parents aren't sparring with one another constantly is still hard to fully comprehend. Yesterday, before and after these comments were cast my direction, we were in fact sparring. I was having a huge dispute with Jeremy about custody modification. We both know that some of the provisions of our custody order need modification, and we both have differing ideas on how to accomplish those goals. On this topic, both of us can go to war like Vikings. But nonetheless, despite our then-existing battle, people—family law professionals, at that—still assumed if we were in the same place speaking to one another, we must be considering reconciliation. Nothing has been farther from the truth, and it is almost entertaining to think anyone would believe such a thing.

For my purposes, that chapter has closed.

I have absolutely no intention of revisiting the problems I fought so hard and diligently to overcome for years. In fact, both of us function better together now that we do not see each other regularly. I spend the time I used to spend arguing doing more productive things. My children are being raised in a calmer and more stable environment both at my home and at Jeremy's home. The distance has been the redeeming aspect of our ability to still do the various jobs we share, and we now do those jobs more effectively as a result. In short, we can't live together anymore, and we both know it. *I do not apologize for my divorce, nor should I have to justify it.* I am a better person without the problems of being married to someone who is not right for me. We aren't bad people for being divorced, but we are incompatible as spouses. However, that does not mean that either of us are so intolerant and angry that we cannot speak civilly. A large part of our civility rests on the fact that we both recognize our incompatibility and choose not to try to change or influence the other person anymore.

Jeremy and I went to counseling at several intervals during our relationship. The problems that plagued our marriage were unique and complicated as are all problems that arise that cause divorce. He and I attempted to save our relationship for years prior to our split with both of us revisiting the same problems over and over. We both choose not to air our "dirty laundry" for the world to see, but I assure you our problems were enough to justify our divorce. I will never give an itemized list of the problems that caused our divorce or the infractions I believe my ex committed. I also know he won't do so either. We are invested in not allowing our children to experience the arguing and destruction that divorces cause, and we are both remorseful that they witnessed our arguing and destructive behaviors prior to our decision to split.

I resent the suggestion of reconciliation by our friends and family. I know in their minds, they believe reconciliation is best for our children. I know that this belief is based on a lack of information about the type of dysfunction our marriage created for our children. Our children are happier and get more of our attention because we aren't together and fighting in their presence. Instead, we have one-on-one time with them without worrying that an argument will interrupt their time with their parents. I also know that the reconciliation advocates usually have good intentions in their suggestions and comments. With those good-intentioned comments comes the feeling that my ex and I are outcasts because of our ability and willingness to remain amicable. The label and perception that all divorced people are angry, resentful and would otherwise reconcile is unfair and misguided. I do not resent Jeremy, and I am not angry with him. The decision to marry and divorce was made by both of us. Both of us made the wrong choice, and we both took turns justifying that choice for too long. I do not blame him for those infractions that caused the divorce because I recognize that I tolerated them. I ignored the very things that made me unhappy along the way to keep the marriage intact until they grew into gargantuan mountains of unhappiness.

A large part of our civility rests on the fact that we both recognize our incompatibility and choose not to try to change or influence the other person anymore.

We saw counselors for three of the eight years we were married. We tried.

I accept responsibility for my own portion of the failure of my marriage. I hope to move forward with

Lifelong Frenemies

that knowledge in mind. I also know that there is no fixing the issues that existed between my ex and me. I also realize that we put on a beautiful display of happiness. Even during the worst parts of our marriage, we kept our problems private. We still keep our problems as co-parents private. However, they exist. Our closest friends and family members tell us how we made the right choice and that we individually seem happier now. In fact, one of our mutual friends and colleagues tells us how she will gladly have lunch with one of us at a time, but not together because she dislikes the way we interact. That interaction in private (the one we don't put on display) is why we are divorced.

Surprisingly, I have not yet had the suggestion that I am seeking reconciliation with my ex from any of my dating partners. Those who have seen us interact understand exactly why we are divorced. To this point, I haven't had someone who was a part of my day-to-day life suggest that I might consider reconciliation or suggest that I try. Typically, these comments come from people who see us on a superficial level. They don't see us interact in an uncontrolled environment.

One of our mutual friends was visiting me at my house when Jeremy stopped by to drop off a file I planned to work on that weekend. He didn't realize that she was visiting when he and I got into an argument on the porch. My friend heard the entire argument and immediately said to me, "I get it now. You two can't see eye to eye on anything."

I was relieved. It can get overwhelming to constantly feel as though people are judging your relationships or lack thereof. It is my opinion that the judgment I have experienced—the comments, the skepticism—all comes from fear. If divorce and/or separation can happen to two people who definitively **don't** hate each other, then it could happen to anyone.

Yes, theoretically it could. I am in the business of divorce and separation, so I see more than my fair share of people ending their relationships. In my experience, divorces and separations are usually a choice both parties are prepared to make. I rarely see a situation in which one spouse is seeking the split and the other is trying to reconcile. And if they are not sure about whether they want to split or the split is one-sided, I refer them to a therapist friend of mine because I don't want to clog the courthouse or my desk with unnecessary "break-up and make-up" paperwork.

Usually, if they drove to my office, paid for parking, took the elevator and sat in my waiting room, they mean business.

They have probably exhausted all possible solutions prior to plunking down a retainer and announcing to the world that they failed at one of the biggest goals they ever had in life. Even in my line of work, knowing most of a couple's personal matters, it is not my right to decide whether the

Lifelong Frenemies

split is in the party's best interests.

In Louisiana, couples with children under 18 have to wait a year before finalizing the divorce. I waited the year during which my ex and I grew from volatile to amicable, and we both still wanted the divorce, *recognizing that we were amicable only as a result of the split.* Typically, these decisions aren't made in haste. So, I assume if you are reading this book, your decision was well considered too. Remind the well-wishers and nay-sayers that you are competent and that the decision to divorce or split from someone is just as personal as the decision to begin the relationship. Would they tell you who to marry? Would you consider their opinion if they did? If not, then they shouldn't tell you who to divorce.

Let It Be

Harmonizing with the Parenting Style of Your Co-Parent

The disputes between co-parents normally arise because of difference of opinions on co-parenting. It is essential that both parents recognize that being the exact same parent is not required nor is it beneficial to the kids. Diversity of parenting styles can benefit the children tremendously. Personally, I have no interest in living in a world where everyone thinks the exact same way as me. I like to expand my thinking and beliefs through interaction with others. I believe that the majority of people feel the same way. I look to reality television as my basis for this belief. I think the attraction to reality television is that the audience can be exposed to the points of view and daily habits of other people without the fear of seeming socially awkward. If I followed a stranger around all day and watched them go to the gym, eat their meals and witness their personal family discussions, I would probably end up with a restraining order for stalking. However, I have watched more episodes of *Keeping Up with the Kardashians* than I am proud to admit. This is because I am drawn to learn more about how other people think and how they choose to live because I recognize that my habits and methods are unique, and I enjoy learning from others' unique methods and habits… in most cases. For the purposes of my co-parenting, I recognize that my ex has unique habits and methods of doing things. Much like the Kardashians, some of these methods and habits are very different than mine. For example, Jeremy grew up in a home with parents who both worked full-time. He believes that being a good parent requires a lot of fun activities outside of the home. He frequently takes the kids on vacations, to the movies and to the zoo.

As a child, Jeremy grew up in a home where his parents traveled with the children frequently, ate every meal in restaurants and were rarely at home. For much of his youth, he attended sleepaway summer camps and had a nanny.

To contrast this, I grew up in a home where my father worked 12-hour days, six days per week and my mother never worked full-time. My parents advocated for me to be a stay-at-home mom

Lifelong Frenemies

for several years after my children were born. We rarely traveled since my father had very limited vacation time. My mother would plan our days with activities in the home because it was difficult for her to bring three children outside of the home by herself. I spent much of my time as a child reading, swimming at the neighborhood pool and playing with my siblings and cousins. During the summers, my family hosted exchange students from France as opposed to traveling abroad.

The varied upbringings that my ex and I experienced have been a source of conflict between us. When we argue (which we inevitably do from time to time), the topic of activities for the kids is a sore spot. Jeremy has expressed that he is the "better" parent because he brings the children places and exposes them to different entertainment opportunities. In my mind, I believe that the children need time to play and unwind at home. Like my mother, I take the children swimming frequently and a large part of our days at home involve imaginative play, such as made-up theatre and dance performances. I recognize that despite our differing parenting styles, both of us turned out to be productive, law-abiding adults.

The beauty of our diverse experiences is that my children are being exposed to both methods of parenting. During the time that they are with their father, the children are largely exposed to an extroverted style of parenting in which they are interacting with the public and being exposed to new environments. They are learning and growing. While they are with me, they are using their imaginations and learning responsibility by helping with the home. I am currently teaching them to play checkers and to ride a bike without training wheels. While this is an introverted style of parenting, I believe it is essential to their growth. They are learning and growing. So, between my ex's parenting style and my parenting style, I feel like the children are receiving a well-rounded upbringing. I often see parenting style differences become an issue for my clients. Significant issues that have surfaced include a heavy exposure to the religion of one parent while the other parent was more spiritual. This is a controversial parenting topic, but one that is very common and difficult to overcome.

It is important to remember that children are miniature adults in training. We as parents are guiding them on a path to make their own choices as adults.

Dietary choices are another issue I see frequently where one parent is exposing the child to a vegetarian or exclusively organic diet and the other parent purchases conventional foods in their home. These issues bring a lot of tension to the co-parenting situation. It is important to remember that the children are miniature adults in training. We as parents are guiding them on a path to make their own choices as adults.

By exposing the children to more choices and various conditions, they are learning about their options, and thereby are in a better position to make better choices.

If dad is a vegetarian, the child may choose to remain a vegetarian after being exposed to the benefits of that choice during his childhood at dad's house. The need to shelter our children from harm also encompasses a requirement that we ourselves do not harm them by failing to respect their opinions and choices.

I look at my parenting journey as a training period—much like attending school.

I am teaching my children life skills and experiences like a math teacher teaches an equation. When they leave their matriculation in the childhood portion of their lives, hopefully, if I did a good job teaching them, they will remember that equation. That doesn't in any respect imply that they will choose to become mathematicians, but I will have equipped them with the basic knowledge necessary to choose that path if they so desire.

For a lot of parents, this perspective may seem exceedingly progressive.

That may be true.

However, the new family structure you are creating is one that was uncommon sixty years ago.

The progression of societal expectations related

to raising children in two homes necessitates a progressive perspective on handling co-parenting issues.

FRENEMY SYNERGY
Working Together to Schedule Custody

Being a single parent, I feel the stress of scheduling conflicts more than anything; carpool, then court, then client meetings, then carpool, then extracurriculars comprise my typical day-to-day schedule. Sometimes these things overlap. On any given day, a 20-minute delay could topple the entire schedule on its face. My mother, who retired from nursing several years ago, often pitches in when the schedule is too burdensome. But sometimes, I need my frenemy to pitch in. My ex and I have a pretty well-drafted and concise custody judgment. There has rarely been a day where we did not know who was caring for the children at any given time. However, things come up that interrupt the ordinary custody schedule. For example, next month, I am traveling to New York to attend a mandatory conference for the American Bar Association. The conference happens to be on the weekend that I have custody of the children. I could ask my mother to watch the kids, but she isn't used to having them for more than a few hours at a time.

So, I am relying on my frenemy to adjust the weekend schedule so I can attend the conference.

In Louisiana, the parties are allowed to agree in writing to issues related to co-parenting without being held in contempt. I always caution my clients that if a modification is ongoing and not a one-time change, it is best to submit a consent judgment to the court to formalize the arrangement. But in cases like my conference where there is an isolated one-time change, the parties can agree in writing to the switch. Jeremy was willing to trade the time for the conference for another weekend to accommodate my business travel plans.

Things change, and issues arise that require you to call in your frenemy for reinforcement.

This is a topic that I frequently address with my clients: the desire to be vindicated and to prevail over your ex hurts the children.

Last week, my ex had a trial early on the docket and asked me to drive our youngest daughter to her summer camp. I had already driven her to accommodate his trial schedule earlier that week, and I was angry with him for failing to thank me for my help. So, I told him no… primarily to spite him. My daughter went to "Before Care" that day instead of having breakfast with me before camp. While nothing in our custody judgment states that I was obligated to take her to camp that day, it would have benefited her to have spent the morning with me as opposed to extending her day at camp. Formal long-term changes to the custody arrangement often creates a huge source of conflict. Depending on your jurisdiction and the type of judgment you have, custody agreements may often be revised to accommodate the changes in the family's time, structure and residency. In most jurisdictions, the courts recognize that over time custody arrangements need to grow with the children. What works for a family with an infant, will not necessarily fit the needs of a family with teenagers.

The desire to be vindicated and to prevail over your ex hurts the children.

Almost half of my custody clients are parents who need to modify an existing custody order to accommodate a material change of circumstance, such as a parent relocation, schedule change for the parents or children, or updating their schedule to better fit their families' needs. Small children who have a parent who lives in another city cannot travel alone to visit their remote parent, but most major airlines allow children to travel alone after the age of eight. I also see cases in which the custody order worked for several years, but the children have extracurricular activities that one parent can accommodate better than the other, resulting in time adjustments that better fit the family's needs.

When these circumstances change, it is important to consult an attorney to make sure you are in accordance with the laws of your state. Those informal conversations that modify the custody arrangement between the parents can lead to a finding of contempt of court depending on the method of communication and the jurisdictional rules related to modification.

This is also one of the biggest sources of discourse between amicable co-parents.

I am currently modifying my custody order with my ex. Despite our normally successful attempts at remaining amicable, negotiations about the judgment changes has sent us both into frenemy mode. Both of us got to the point where we exchanged potential motions we planned to file in the court and attorneys we intended to hire to represent us.

Then a couple of days into our dispute, my ex randomly pulled up behind me in traffic, so I flipped him the middle finger through my sunroof and laughed hysterically… he responded the same way, and we called a truce for a few days.

By stepping away from the agreement for a few days to recollect our thoughts, we can keep our amicability intact and also come up with a more

Lifelong Frenemies

effective strategy to resolve the issues.

I tell my clients pretty often that half of my job is taking the emotion out of the client's case. Clients who visit me, with rare exception, are hurt, angry and often overly emotional. Ending a relationship with your significant other is hard enough without the logistics of co-parenting. My job as a family law attorney is not only to advise my clients on the law, but also to help them move forward in a reasonable manner. If a client is exceptionally unreasonable, they are likely to be viewed as unwilling to work with the other parent, which affects their credibility with the court. Most attorneys hire other attorneys to represent them in their own cases because they recognize that there is a substantial likelihood that they will become too emotionally involved to be effective. I have not yet had the occasion where I needed to hire another attorney, but the other day, I thought that would change.

My immature exchange in traffic was just the trick to bring humor to a tense situation and let the tension retreat.

I find that stepping away from the issues, even for a short period of time, diffuses the situation effectively. I would love to say that my ex and I are true friends and that we don't fight about trivial issues, but that is not true. We fight, and we fight hard! We use the "seafood on the countertop" rule to maintain our frenemy relationship. Sometimes, the space we take before revisiting a topic in dispute is longer than predicted, and that is okay. I usually test the waters by trying to gauge the mood. I am not bringing up our custody issues if I can tell my ex is under stress or has had a bad day. Typically, I wait until something good happens or there is a funny moment before deciding to bring up the topic in dispute. Adjusting custody arrangements is always difficult. Currently, my ex and I have agreed to break up the holiday visitation in a more effective way so that the holidays alternate during each season. We cannot agree on the weekly schedule.

> *I am not bringing up our custody issues if I can tell my ex is under stress or has had a bad day.*

Both of us are trained in family law litigation and mediation. I have served as a child custody visitation mediator, and I am listed on the Louisiana Arbitration section panel of child custody mediators, but I am still struggling to resolve this dispute because I am emotionally involved in the outcome.

Stepping away and even consulting a less interested person in their opinion of the situation can be invaluable in remaining reasonable in the resolution of disputes between co-parents. The difference between my reasonable clients and non-reasonable clients are vast. Those clients who recognize that remaining reasonable is in the best interests of their children save themselves a lot of stress and money in litigating their disputes. That being said, I myself periodically get further away from reason than I should. Children are the most important people in our lives. The love we have for our children is unconditional and greater than any other love possible because they are a part of ourselves. That complicates our ability to remain objective.

It is hard to see that those children are still people in their own right, and their desires should be considered.

For the most part, children love both of their parents and prefer to be equally involved in both parent's lives. Keeping that perspective in mind can help co-parents work to amicably solve custody adjustments in a manner that benefits both parents as well as the children.

THE DOG ATE MY HOMEWORK
Two-House Parenting Problems

As I am writing, I recently picked my youngest daughter up from summer camp for my summer visitation weekend. I am really unhappy with the changes I see as a result of her six weeks (so far) with her father. She has clearly picked up some weight and seems to be completely off of her bedtime schedule. I am going to have my work cut out for me this weekend only to send her back to her dad's to relearn the routine in his home. I just spent an hour explaining to my daughter that I will not put on the television program she wants until she first watches the educational program I selected. This created an hour-long hissy fit. Then I served her chicken, edamame and watermelon slices, and she asked if she could have cereal for dinner. It is clear she has learned a new routine in her extended visitation with her dad, and I am less than thrilled.

This is going to be hard work for me to fix. I only have her for the weekend, and I already see that the rules my ex has in place in his home have become the "new normal". Fixing it this weekend would be futile since she will be with him for another two weeks. So, I am planning my back-to-school boot camp: bedtime routines, dinnertime and discipline are all going to need adjustment.

When she left for the summer, I had all of these routines down to a science.

I tried to explain my routines to Jeremy, but obviously that had no effect. I will be undoing the majority of the summer throughout the month of August in preparation for the new school year, and I am pretty pissed off about it. So, I hit Pinterest for dinner ideas, exercise activities for kids and daily schedules. I love Pinterest for things related to home organization and kid-friendly planning. Also, I can find pins on Pinterest that I think are relevant and send them to Jeremy. I am furiously planning the "welcome-home-clean-up routine" that has become the norm every summer after the kids return from their dad's house.

Another issue that really "frosts my muffins" is the homework/bed/bath routine during the school year. I run a pretty tight ship. Bedtime is at 8:30

every night with no TV in bed. Jeremy lets the kids watch TV in bed, and every Thursday night after spending their weekly Wednesday with their dad, they give me trouble for not allowing the TV to be on in the bedroom.

Sometimes, they come home from their Dad's with their hair unbrushed or without having had a bath the night before. It is frustrating because all of that falls on me. So, Wednesday night—when their dad has them, I usually relax, recharge and prepare for the rest of the week. However, it turns out to create even more work when the kids get home on Thursday after school. They argue with me about staying awake later, eating their home-cooked dinner (as opposed to restaurant-made) and watching TV in the bed.

This is a part of the two-home parenting that I still struggle with. I would be lying if I said that there is a quick fix for the management of the two-home, two-rules situation. *Communication helps, but only if your co-parent is willing to implement the plans and decisions that you have discussed.*

In my case, these things usually start off with the best intentions, but the follow-up falls through the cracks. Further, this issue is the number one reason I see clients return to my office for custody modifications. Usually, one parent has complaints about the level of effort the other parent is putting into some aspect of the child's life. Whether it is that the child stopped regularly attending sports practice while in the other parent's care or the co-parent is not preparing the child adequately for school, I see parents complaining about the disparities in the two households as the primary reason for their disputes on a regular basis. Ultimately, each parent has their own parenting style. However, certain routines should transcend between the homes. The most important routine that I believe should be uniform among the two homes is the bedtime routine. If the child is going to sleep at 8 p.m. in one home and 10 p.m. in the other, the parents will have a difficult time adhering to either bedtime since the child's internal clock cannot adjust every few days. In this situation, I would recommend discussing a mutually feasible time to put the child to bed in both homes so that there is consistency. Consistency is key.

> *The most important routine that I believe should be uniform among the two homes is the bedtime routine.*

As discussed in prior chapters, the goal is to provide as much stability and routine as possible in light of the changing and new family structure.

The more cohesive a child's routine is, the better they can adjust to the two-home family.

Additionally, the rules must be similar in both homes. If a child has performed poorly in school and is grounded in one home, the other home should honor the discipline system of the home that initiated the punishment for the infraction.

Children should not be allowed to circumvent their obligations as a result of the custody exchange. I also see parents who intentionally attempt to be the "good" parent or the "fun" parent in an effort to gain the greater admiration of the child.

This is a slippery slope where the child eventually suffers.

Regardless of the momentary enjoyment of the rule-bending home, the child is experiencing the instability of the two-home parenting and consistency is lost. If the goal is to create responsible and accountable adults, then teaching that responsibility and accountability will be expected in both homes and only benefits the child in the long run.

Today, I had a pretty nasty argument with my ex related to custody modifications we were interested in making. He said at one point (in an effort to bolster his relatively weak argument) that my older daughter doesn't want to live with me because my house is no fun. I had to remind him that she is a child and that the decision of where to live is out of her hands, but additionally, she cannot be permitted to dodge responsibility and discipline by flip-flopping between our homes.

Presenting a united front on the core parenting values and standing up for one another's rules prevents the child from learning to use the system to break the rules. So, there should be no incident of, *"You may be grounded at dad's house, but you aren't here at mine."* Parents should discuss the big decisions about discipline and rules and follow through with them in both homes to encourage the accountability that is expected of adults. Unfortunately, this doesn't always play out as well as suggested. I typically resort to the "this is my house, and these are my rules" policy when my attempts at consistency fail.

I look at the situation like this: In Louisiana, I am allowed to bring alcoholic beverages on the street as long as they are contained in a plastic container, but this is not so in Washington, D.C. I was in law school in D.C.; I stepped out of a staffer party on Capitol Hill with a red, solo cup full of beer and started walking towards my dorm with my roommate then.

She said to me, "What. Are. You. Doing. With. That. Beer?!"

I replied, "Drinking it while I walk back to campus..."

I was then informed promptly about open container laws of D.C. that did not exist in Louisiana. Apparently, despite the fact that I was over the age of 21 and had my beer in a plastic container, it was illegal for me to drink on the street in D.C. I was shocked!

So, I treat my rules like the laws of D.C. and Louisiana. What you are allowed to do at dad's house, you cannot do here. Sorry, you will be in trouble. Those are the rules of my jurisdiction. In my jurisdiction, my home, the rules I made apply. Generally, the rules are quite similar. For example, serious infractions like bank robbery are still a crime in D.C. and Louisiana without question. But the open container law is quite different and much less serious. I expect a small amount of minor infractions to my rules as a result of the children being in another jurisdiction (Jeremy's house) for a large portion of their youth. However, for the *big* infractions, we have to be on the same page.

Skipping school is one of those *big* infractions. Jeremy and I would both agree that it is a high crime, and we would be pretty consistent about enforcing the resulting punishment. We agree that the big stuff needs to be discussed.

On the contrary, my ex and I often disagree on the handling of minor infractions like backtalk and hissy fits. I think he overreacts when he should ignore the behavior. I believe that if the children do not get attention for (minor) bad behavior, it will often correct itself. Jeremy is a fan of time-outs, while I walk away from the hissy fit and inform the children that I won't entertain their behavior.

Jurisdictions in the law vary on laws and enforcement just like homes vary with differing parenting styles. I try to keep in mind that the children are expected to plan accordingly for their environment. This is the case when they visit their grandparents, school, and friends' homes. Each household has its own culture and rules. I try to respect my ex's household culture and rules to the extent that it does not spill over onto my household culture and rules. But this is one of my biggest struggles mostly because the children learn the habits and routines and they are difficult to adjust.

OTHER MOTHERING BOTHER FATHERING
Handling Out-Laws and Partners

So, your ex found a new partner. Great! Now she or he can address all those issues your ex has that drove you insane for the duration of your past relationship. Good luck with that… (See Chapter Six). But now, this new dating partner wants to express their opinions in your child's life. They may think you need to change some of your parenting ways. They may do what I call "Other Mother" you. In the case of dads, I call it "Bother Father." It is what happens when another person (not the child's parent) attempts to assume the role of the parent and steps on your toes by asserting their opinion where it is not welcome. Here are some examples: *"Did your mom really give you water in a plastic bottle? Doesn't she care about BPAs? Here, sweetie. Grandma has a glass bottle for you to use."*

Boom! You have been "**Other Mothered!**"

"Now that I'm your stepfather, I think you should call me 'Pop-Pop.'"
Nope! You just got **"Bother Fathered!"**

Other mothering and bother fathering is counterproductive to creating a healthy two-home family. In order to maintain and encourage your co-parent's peaceful cooperation, this sort of behavior will naturally create an environment where your co-parent feels that their role is being threatened. This will put your co-parent in fight-or-flight mode where they feel the need to either assert their dominant role in the position of parent or alternatively, they throw their hands up and quit to the detriment of the children. The primary responsibility for preventing this type of behavior falls on the parent most closely associated with the annoying offender. I always look at degrees of association between disputing people to determine if the relationship has a third-party intervenor that has contributed to the problem in some way.

If a third-party has made unwelcome remarks or engaged in negative behavior with your co-parent, there is a substantial likelihood that you have not communicated to the offending person that the priority is to effectively co-parent and that goal is a top priority to you. Usually, with rare exceptions, when your loved ones believe you have a desire or

Lifelong Frenemies

goal in life, they behave in a manner that does not infringe upon you achieving that goal. If your goals are consistently intercepted by the behaviors of your loved ones, most people will modify the terms of the relationship in order to bypass the problem and reach the goals despite the resistance from loved ones.

It is important that you express to your loved ones that despite the problems that arose ancillary to the breakup, your relationship with your co-parent has been modified and has not terminated completely. Communicate to your loved ones that the relationship is now one of teamwork toward a common goal of raising healthy, well-adjusted children, and that these new relationship roles are challenging and new to you and your co-parent as well.

Most importantly, it is *essential* that your loved ones understand that the problems which arose during the break up between you and your ex have nothing to do with the children and that they do not deserve to be put in the middle of their parents.

By requesting that your loved ones understand your feelings and the feelings of your children in advance of their interactions with your co-parent, you are likely to be successful in preventing the majority of the problems that may arise.

If circumstances are such that the hostility between your co-parent and your loved ones is overwhelming, the easiest short-term solution is to interact with them separately.

For example, I often have clients who ask their new partners to perform custody exchanges and make phone calls to the co-parent when the parent is working or otherwise unavailable. This is a lose-lose scenario. First, the scenario is often caused by the new partner's insecurities related to the co-parent still remaining in the lives of the parent and children.

If you choose to date a partner who has insecurities related to your co-parent that interfere with the co-parenting goals you have for your children, that is a discussion you and your partner should have separate from your co-parent and children.

The lack of security in your current relationship should not negatively affect the other relationships in your life. If it does and you choose to continue that relationship, it will be detrimental to your children and new family structure.

Likewise, your co-parent should refrain from reminiscing on your relationship and comparing it to your relationship with your new partner. I reference the first chapter of this book where I stress that the romantic relationship between the co-parents must be completely over for effective co-parenting to work. This is the time to reflect upon all of the things that caused the breakup and recall how hard you both worked to overcome those issues.

I remember one time I had to bring the children their security blankets at their father's home. My ex and my new partner had been getting along very well and had even spent time together with our mutual friends. It was storming, and I was at my home with my new partner. It was no trouble to drop them off, so we went together to his home. Upon exchanging the children's blankets, my ex made an inappropriate comment about our former intimate life and reminisced about the rainy days we had spent together during our relationship. I quickly left with my partner and apologized for my ex's inappropriate comment. Their relationship was never quite the same.

The next day, after I had managed my partner's anger regarding my ex's comments, I called my ex to discuss it. I let him know that I was unhappy with the comment and that I thought it was inappropriate. I also asked that, in the future, he respect my partner's feelings as I try to respect his partner's feelings. I also bought the children blankets to keep at their father's home so that the scenario wouldn't reoccur.

Since that time, he has not made any other inappropriate remarks. While he didn't see the harm in the comment, he stated he did not mean to be disrespectful and would be more considerate in the future. I thought to myself and also told my partner, "It is comments like that which display how terribly ill-fitting we were as a couple."

Sometimes, it is a good thing your ex reminds you of all the differences that exist in your personalities and ideologies. It is hard to be a single parent and even harder to explain how you can remain friends with your ex, but you cannot reconcile.

When it comes to the details and hurtful behaviors that happened during the breakup, it is best to forgive, but not forget.

Also, for the purpose of maintaining your amicability with your co-parent and still having a healthy relationship with your new partner, I always think it is best to discuss these issues with your new partner prior to introducing him or her to your ex.

In-laws often present challenges as well. My former mother-in-law was one who could criticize you by issuing what seemed to be a compliment. An example of the type of thing she would say is, *"Did you cut your hair yourself? It is so unique!"*

Normally, coming from anyone else, a comment like that would receive complete dismissal because I don't really care what other people think of me. But when my ex and I were still together, it was just the sort of comment that would put me in a bad mood for days while I waited for availability at the most expensive salon in town.

My ex saw no harm in these kinds of statements, assuming it was a compliment and complaining about the salon bill.

So, we fought. We fought because I cared.

I cared what his mother thought. I cared that he did not notice that her statement was hurtful. I cared that the statement had the capacity to hurt me because my relationship with her mattered.

Today, I am divorced. I am not building the same kind of relationship with my ex's family. I am being civil and coexisting because caring about the opinion of his family and building a close relationship with them is no longer a goal. The goal is to facilitate a working relationship from which my children can benefit. Our differing opinion about my hairstyle has nothing to do with my kids. The problem arises when third-parties, ie. new dating partners and former in-laws, decide to criticize the other parent to the co-parent and children. This is a horrible situation for all parties involved, especially the children. It is important that you communicate to your family and dating partners that criticism of the other parent to the children is not in their best interest.

The goal is to facilitate a working relationship from which my children can benefit.

Third-parties often mistakenly believe that they will be able to exert some influence on the child's opinion of their parent by speaking poorly about the parent to the children. This, more likely than not, will result in the child losing respect for the third-party and becoming defensive of that parent.

In most cases, the child's extended family has the child's best interest at heart. Often times, the critical third-party recognizes that this sort of criticism is detrimental to their relationship with the child. However, the child typically benefits from having supportive and caring extended family.

Parents as well as extended family members should recognize that the child has experienced a traumatic family transition.

Maintaining a harmonious and stable environment for the child allows the child to adjust in a more productive manner to the new family dynamics. It is essential that the adult immediate and extended family members prioritize the feelings of the child, who often cannot express their emotions in a meaningful way. **By engaging in negative talk about the co-parent, children experience heightened awareness of the negative aspects of the family transition post-parental separation.** While the adult immediate and extended family members are experiencing their own personal strife related to the parental separation, the children are more closely affected and are less able to find productive outlets to express the stress associated with the family transition. When the adult family members, whom the children rely upon to provide security and support, increase stress by speaking negatively about the co-parent, the children are adversely affected because the consistency of the security and support is compromised.

In my cases, I typically include the Louisiana Standard Co-Parenting Guidelines in my custody consent judgments. One of the most essential

Lifelong Frenemies

co-parenting guidelines, in my opinion, states that, "Neither parent shall say anything in the presence of the minor children that would diminish the child's love and affection for the other parent, and they shall not allow third-parties to do so either (St. Philip v. Montalbano, 2013)."

When I see clients who have experienced a violation of this guideline by their co-parent or their co-parent's friends and families, they are usually irate and unwilling to work with the other party to agree on the details of their custody arrangements. The child, who hears the negative commentary about the parent they love, experiences not only the negative commentary and insecurity that accompanies those comments, but also suffers the negative effects of parents who are unwilling to work together for the child's best interest. So, that child will likely be the child who can't have both parents attend their extracurricular activities, birthday parties or other experiences, unlike children of married parents.

Last week, my daughter came home from sleep-away camp for a few days. She celebrated her birthday at camp and my parents planned a tea party the day she returned. My father and ex-husband do not get along. Privately and exclusively, both of them have told me how happy they are that they no longer have to spend time with one another. However, during the tea party, they talked about my daughter's experiences at camp and made small pleasantries. Both my ex-husband and my father are aware that my daughters love both of them and that they are happiest when everyone is together and getting along.

Independently, my father and ex-husband have seen each other in the grocery store, glanced at each other and each walked the other way. However, when the children are watching, they manage to make enough small talk that the environment is harmonious and stable for the kids. I couldn't be prouder of them both. Their expression of compassion was not directed at one another, but instead at the children. They both communicated unconditional love of my daughters that afternoon.

I often see the most trouble with these interactions with new dating partners. The new dating partner often feels threatened by the history between their partner and the co-parent. This is understandable since the new partners are struggling to build a foundation in their relationship and define their level of commitment.

It is essential that the communication lines be open between both partners as well as with the co-parent. When my ex-husband met his current partner and it became evident that it would be a lasting relationship, the three of us had lunch. I won't pretend that the lunch was the most comfortable interaction I've ever had. It was sort of like introducing an older pet to a new pet. We immediately sized each other up to determine the threat level. I stoically

Lifelong Frenemies

informed Jeremy's new dating partner that I would be completely supportive of their relationship, but that I was to not be undermined as a parent. His dating partner carefully "fork-fed" salad to my ex as a gesture of possessiveness. It was awkward, but necessary. We both

The goal is to maintain the environment that the children have experienced prior to the introduction of a new dating partner and siblings.

took the opportunity to assert our "ground rules." I was not to be usurped from my parental role, and his new partner was not to be usurped from her romantic role. I was comfortable with the unspoken deal we negotiated, and we have been great friends since that lunch. I find that this situation is more problematic with younger couples and co-parents. I believe this is due to the substantial likelihood that the new couple will also have children who will become the children's siblings. In an effort to construct consistency between the children and the new siblings, there is often a discrepancy between the way the two households function, and that becomes a point of contention in how the new siblings are raised.

In this situation, I typically see the co-parents warring over the co-parenting influences of the children in the household with new siblings. In these cases, it is imperative that the household containing new siblings accommodates the children despite the influences of the co-parent's household demeanor. Keeping in mind that the children's stability is the most important factor to raise happy, well-adjusted children, the goal is to maintain the environment that the children have experienced prior to the introduction of a new dating partner and siblings.

The parent must take caution to facilitate a situation where the new dating partner is able to understand that their relationship includes the children. This requires carefully choosing a dating partner and effective communication between the couple related to the children and co-parent.

I have represented clients who have left communication with the co-parent exclusively to the new dating partner. While there is a sense of security about the new relationship when all communication and custody exchanges between the co-parents are filtered or facilitated through the new dating partner, this type of scenario is highly problematic. Though, in theory, it secures the dating partner from concerns that the interactions of the co-parents could result in reunification, the reality is that the co-parenting becomes ineffective and the children suffer as a result. The children often see the new dating partner as a threat and the parent as disinterested. This places the co-parent in a defensive position as well since the perception is that the new dating partner is acting as a parent,

Lifelong Frenemies

thus potentially usurping their role.

I strongly advise my clients against these types of arrangements. In Louisiana, third-parties have significantly diminished custody rights in comparison to parents. In Louisiana, cases where a dating partner, stepparent or grandparent is providing the majority of the childcare and co-parenting communication, I am often able to increase visitation for the co-parent based on the parent's consistent unavailability. In addition, the children become aware that the parent is unavailable and become resentful, creating an environment of instability.

When handling the third-parties in your child's life, it is best for the children that they see others being respectful of both of their parents. The children will gain consistency, stability and respect for both parents. As a co-parent, it is important that the third-parties you choose to have in your child's life prioritize the child's best interest as well as your best interest as both you and your child transition into your new family environment.

Paper Chasing

Managing Child Support and Expenses

First thing I usually hear from the parent who pays child support that comes into my office is that they feel that their child support payment is not going toward the children. I usually ask, "Has the light bill been paid? Are there groceries in the pantry? Was there gas in the car to get the children to school?" These are all things that child support helps pay. Many parents believe that child support should go exclusively to toys, clothes and outings for the children, but this is not the reason for child support. Child support exists to provide a similar experience for the children in both parent's homes. The courts do not want the children leaving mom's mansion to have visitation with dad in his shack. This is the reason for diversity in child support awards. The award of child support is based upon the number of children in the family and the discrepancy between the parents in incomes.

Inevitably, the children should not feel a huge change between the two households because it is not in their best interests. In my situation, my ex and I do the same job in the same community, so child support is largely based on the increased amount of time that I have the children. Since I have them more frequently, the costs are greater to maintain their lifestyle in my home than in his, so he pays child support despite our similarity in earning capacity.

It is important not to spoil the children with gifts and activities to try to compensate for the thing the children really need—quality time with both parents.

Despite all of this knowledge, my ex and I still fight about money.

Who paid for the children's school registration fees this year?

Who is claiming the children as dependents on the tax returns?

These are all issues that come up in co-parenting relationships. I am fortunate that Jeremy tends to be very generous with paying child support and the majority of the children's additional expenses.

Lifelong Frenemies

Disputes still arise though because we both want the best for our children, and the best is expensive.

All parents experience some degree of guilt related to their separation. It is important not to spoil the children with gifts and activities to try to compensate for the thing the children really need—quality time with both parents. Whether that quality time is at an amusement park or at a public library is truly unimportant. What matters is that the children are happy and have an opportunity to experience both parents' influence.

I discussed earlier in this book how my parenting style differs from my ex's parenting style, but money should not be a factor in the ability for either parent to provide for their children.

In reality, money is always a factor, and child support is the method by which the family law courts attempt to equalize that situation. Even after separation, former romantic partners who share children can expect some degree of arguments to be based on finances since finances affect the lives of the children.

Whenever there is an opportunity to do so, co-parents should share expenses related to the children. My ex and I share a zoo membership and neighborhood swim club. Anytime there is an ability to join an organization as a "family" we share the expense as opposed to purchasing two memberships. The money saved by joining these organizations together means that we can afford to join more organizations and our children can participate in more activities than if we had to pay for two households every time.

If at any time the children are not being supported properly by the child support recipient parent, in most states, an attorney can request an accounting of the amounts used for the children from the child support payment. I have requested child support accounting in cases where it is clear the recipient is not spending child support responsibly and the basic needs of the children are not being met.

However, if both households are providing the same or similar lifestyles for the children, a child support accounting is not necessary.

Child support is also subject to adjustment. If one of the co-parents has a change in income or begins cohabitating with someone who relieves their obligations, then child support modification is often necessary to re-equalize the homes. I see this a lot when one parent loses their job, or a parent remarries. Another issue I see a lot in my office is when one parent seeks to modify custody to avoid paying child support. I strongly feel that if the sole motivation for increasing custody is financial, that parent is not considering the needs of the children.

I always strive to provide what my parents provided to me for my children. Generally, my upbringing was pretty grounded. I had what I needed, but I wasn't spoiled and I feel that has benefitted me as an adult. When I am able to make purchases

Lifelong Frenemies

or plan vacations that I wouldn't have been given by my parents, I feel as though I have achieved some level of success as an adult. It is my hope that my lifestyle will be exceeded by my children, so I try to keep their lifestyle as children reasonable for them to exceed as adults.

I believe that keeping their expectations reasonable at this point allows them to grow as life progresses and also gives them the desire to attain success. With that in mind, both co-parents should be on the same page as to the level of lifestyle they want to provide for their children. There should not be a huge discrepancy between the households. **Buying a child's affections through lavish gifts and activities communicates that material things equal love, and this can cause problems in their adult life.** At the end of the parenting journey, the goal is to have raised productive and well-adjusted adults.

Determining where to send the children to school is another issue I see frequently in my practice. In New Orleans (where my office is located), there are more private schools per capita than anywhere else in the world. Many of my clients have disputes over where to send the children to school because of the rising tuition costs at those schools. Determining how to pool resources in the best interests of your child is another issue that requires amicability. *Generally, if a child is performing well in an educational environment, it is best not to disrupt that environment.*

Most importantly, finances are enhanced after the children reach the age of majority. College expenses are soaring, and more students are taking student loans to fund their education than ever before. While child support awards generally do not exceed the age of 18, parents can often extend the financial support of children beyond the requirements set forth in the child support laws. I have had cases where clients included college expenses in a consent judgment, and I recommend that in cases where the children intend to go to college.

I had a friend growing up whose father, an extremely successful physician, financially terminated the children at age of majority. The oldest daughter was admitted to a highly-ranked college in the Northeast. She worked as a lifeguard and her mother took an extra job to help fund what wasn't covered by scholarships. She ended her relationship with her father as a result, viewing his decision as punitive to her for her close relationship with her mother.

I feel that if a parent can help ensure the success of their children and the children show promise of attaining that success, the parents should make every effort to support them to the best of their abilities. Many colleges and private schools base financial aid on the combined income of the parents. This can be devastating to a two-family child where the more affluent parent is not contributing to the child's education. In many cases, the financial aid calculation does not reflect the child's actual ability to pay out of pocket for tuition and fees.

This is an important issue to keep in mind when discussing college expenses with your co-parent. If parents can help their children, regardless of their financial ability to provide, the effort should not be retracted out of spite for the other parent. The needs of the children do not go away because of the parents' separation.

Communicating your financial goals for the children with your ex is essential to providing a consistent and beneficial upbringing to the children, regardless of the standard provided.

For those single parents struggling to financially provide for their children, access the resources available to you in your city. There are several resources available that are often underutilized to provide an excellent education to your children. In addition to being an attorney, I am a librarian. Public libraries are underused resources for providing education. The interlibrary loan program through the Library of Congress allows public libraries to transfer books between libraries when a work is not in stock at the library closest to the patron.

In addition, the Library of Congress has digitized several popular books into e-books, allowing widespread access through their website. Libraries aren't limited to books anymore either. Many public libraries offer free access to college courses through podcasts, movie rentals, lectures, foreign language courses and even homework assistance. Lack of funding should never be a reason for diminishing a child's education.

Also, many cities offer free extracurricular activities to families regardless of financial need. In New Orleans and many other major cities, government-sponsored recreation programs and nonprofits offer sports, swimming lessons, summer camps and even music lessons at no cost or discounted rates.

A few summers ago, my daughter took ballet through the city recreational department for free. In fact, that class was provided by the local professional ballet association, which otherwise only offers classes to adults. In that instance, the free course my daughter attended was a better course than what would have been available through a private ballet academy.

Free resources for education are more available to parents now than ever before. The ability to access information on the internet has brought education to a new level.

Even schools like Harvard, Georgetown and Cornell offer free podcasts of their college-level courses to the public on the internet.

While this is no replacement for the finances that are necessary through equitable child support, there are several resources that assist parents regardless of financial need who are working to raise a brilliant child. I access these resources for

Lifelong Frenemies

my children, and I encourage all parents to do the same. A list of resources for education, child support and co-parenting assistance is included at the end of this book.

10

Burnt Pancakes

Handling Holidays Together and Separately

Holidays are one of the most stressful times for co-parents. I see the majority of my business peak after the holidays and summer visitation periods because of the stress from vacations, extended family influences and difficulties during holiday custody exchanges. These exchanges typically do not involve the co-parents exclusively, and the presence of extended family members, who aren't used to participating in a custody exchange or sharing a holiday with the co-parent, influence the mood of the holiday. A turkey that finally hit the table later than expected could become a point of contention when the co-parent arrives for the scheduled custody exchange. Grandma might not understand why the co-parent has to take the child when the turkey just came out of the oven, and the co-parent may not be able to accommodate the delay. In many families, this is just the sort of scenario that can escalate into the courthouse.

It is important to keep in mind that the holidays are a stressful time for people who get along easily. Now you are trying to manage the holidays with a former romantic partner, with whom you share a child. Things can escalate quickly. The most important thing to plan for during the holiday custody exchanges is third-party influences. You are gathered with your family and friends who likely haven't interacted with your ex much since the breakup; they have an opinion of your ex, they took a side during your arguments and they have an opinion now. The goal is to keep those opinions and interactions civil until the child is exchanged.

Typically, the first year of separation is when tension is the highest, and diffusing the situation often takes time.

Gauge the mood of the gathering, and try to determine in advance whether it is better for the exchange to occur at a neutral place away from the family gathering or at the gathering itself.

I would recommend that parents begin their first separate holiday season doing exchanges in a neutral location as opposed to the location of the holiday gathering. Typically, the first year of separation is when tension is the highest, and diffusing the situation often takes time.

If at all possible, I recommend alternating holidays as opposed to exchanging during the holiday itself as it allows each parent to experience the full holiday with the child. Every family is different. When drafting a holiday custody proposal, my first goal is to determine which holidays each parent celebrates. In my custody arrangement, I have Christmas every year even though I am Jewish because my extended family is Christian, and Jeremy's family does not celebrate Christmas. Jeremy has the children every New Year because his family typically vacations during that time and they like to bring the children along. Winter break works out very nicely for our co-parenting situation because our families celebrate opposite holidays.

Another consideration I usually inquire about with my clients is their holiday traditions. Is there a family party on Christmas Eve? Does the family attend services at a particular time?

If there are firmly-held family traditions, the custody schedule can be customized in many cases to accommodate both families' needs.

Children's birthdays are another source of stress. In many cases, each parent fights for the major birthday years, 5, 10, 15... I always recommend both parents attending the child's birthday party if it is feasible. Since my divorce, my ex and I have been able to co-host every birthday for our children.

One year, after a dispute between us over party details, I got so annoyed that I bought my daughter a toy piano since the party was at his house.

He immediately looked at me as she opened it and said, "Nice! I bet I know who bought that."

Yep! I did because every parent knows there is no toy more annoying than a musical instrument in the hands of a three-year-old.

Petty, but effective, and the piano is still at his house!

The next year, he gave her play dough at my house because play dough in the carpet takes hours to clean.

Despite our toy wars, we have civilly attended and planned every birthday party since our divorce. The first party was awkward. Our mutual friends seemed slightly frightened to attend a party with both of us post-divorce, but after an hour or so, the mood lightened significantly. The important thing we conveyed at the party was that it was our daughter's day. She wanted both of her parents there, and that was the most important thing to both of us. We can argue any day, but after the split, our daughter deserved to put that out of her mind and celebrate with both of us.

The most difficult holiday I have celebrated since my split was the first night of Passover after my divorce. I converted to Judaism a few years before I got married and had not spent a Jewish holiday alone before. Though I knew friends who would gladly accept me at their celebrations, I knew that I was not good company and ended up celebrating the holiday by myself in my living room while my children spent the holiday with their father and his new partner. It was difficult, but empowering to me at the time to be alone with my thoughts and commit to pursuing this holiday with or without my children, who are now the only members of my family who share my faith.

Regardless of your cultural background, celebrating the holidays without your children for the first time is particularly stressful. Keeping the company of friends and family can help reduce the inevitable resentment that comes from feeling like you are alone on the holidays without your children. I frequently choose to travel when it is my ex's holiday visitation. Something about being somewhere else keeps me from feeling the urge to cook and decorate that most parents feel on any given holiday. Whether you go on a legitimate vacation or simply pack a bag and crash on a friend's couch (both of which I have done), not being home during my "off" holidays seem to take away the sting of loneliness that creeps in during those times.

The important thing is that both parents try to keep the children's routine as normal as possible.

If the children ask to call or see the other parent on a holiday, the co-parent should try to accommodate the children's wishes.

To this day, I still help my children make cards

and gifts for my ex and his family on the holidays where gifts are exchanged. Despite the fact that I never liked that particular sister-in-law, I stuff glitter and cut out pieces of paper into their carry-on bag every year for Hanukah. My kids need to feel like they participated in gift-giving, despite my feelings about any particular person involved.

Mother's Day is another holiday that annoys the tar out of me as a single mother. Every year, I wake up to my girls, who are too little to understand what Mother's Day is about and curse my ex under my breath when I see my married friends on Facebook with their homemade cards and pancakes. My parents have brought me flowers every year since my divorce and usually by noon, my ex shows up at my house with some little gift and a thank you for being the mother of his kids.

But nothing replaces burnt Mother's Day pancakes...especially when it has been harder to be a mother since I have been a single mom than when

I got my burnt pancakes in the past.

Bah humbug!

Only a few more years until my older daughter can finally burn the pancakes by herself!

I try to look on the bright side with the single parent holiday dilemma. On the one hand, the holiday chaos is split in half. I have half the cooking and cleaning to do every year.

On the other hand, I miss the burnt pancakes and the fireworks every New Years' Eve. With the

Lifelong Frenemies

holidays, it is important to adapt because the faster you adapt to the new situation, the faster your children will adapt.

11

Your House Sucks

Managing Temper Tantrums During Custody Exchanges

I never thought in a million years that my daughter would tell me she "hates me" and "never wants to be by me again" until I got divorced. The sweet little angel who lights up like a sparkler when I pick her up from school cut me like a knife one Sunday afternoon when her father brought her home. Within an eight-hour timeframe, she went from "I hate your house" to "Mommy, can I live with you forever?" Custody exchanges are hard on the children. Tonight, I met my ex in the driveway to give him a file for a trial he is covering for me in the morning, and my daughter was in the backseat. As he drove off, I could hear her crying to stay with me. I assured her that we would snuggle tomorrow night and kissed her goodbye. Even a brief exchange with the children can trigger stress for them.

My ex and I sometimes have breakfast with our kids on Sundays before they go to religious school because the exchange is easier at school. We both try to spend some time with the kids together so that they can feel like we still get along, and there is some ease to the separation in their minds. But when the time comes for one parent to leave the children with the other, tantrums result. One parent feels like the monster abandoning the kids, and the other feels like the unwanted and unloved parent. My ex is particularly skilled at playing these tantrums to his favor.

When he is the parent leaving, "Look how much they love me; I'm the best!"

When I am the parent leaving, "See, they'd rather be with you, so you should take them."

Ugh...*frenemies*!

I'm glad he can put a positive outlook to the situation, but in reality, neither of us wants to be the parent who drives off while the children protest, and neither of us wants to be the parent who feels inadequate. I cannot stress enough how much parents should refrain from discussing potential custody adjustments in front of the kids.

Not only do you want to be consistent with the schedule so that they feel more secure with the new situation, but the last thing you want to do is to allow the tantrum to prevail and inform the child that they are in control of the situation if they behave poorly.

My ex and I used to exchange the children on Sunday evenings at 6 p.m., and many of the custody orders I negotiate have Sunday exchanges. I found that, for me, school exchanges were much easier. When the kids have the whole day at school to transition from one parent's home to the other's, the transition is a lot smoother than when the exchanges are at a parent's home. The Sunday breakfast routine works too because we both take them to religious school, and then the custodial parent of the day picks them up seamlessly. Both my ex and I have struggled with the exchanges.

I cannot stress enough how much parents should refrain from discussing potential custody adjustments in front of the kids.

We have both been the recipient of the emotional thrashing that our children inflict due to the stress they experience during home exchanges. For the most part, our kids are happier when they are settled post-exchange than when we were married because they get more exclusive time with each of us. We aren't talking to each other when we are with them, so they get to be the center of attention during each of our custodial times. But, the custody exchanges at each other's homes throw everything for a loop. As family law attorneys, neither my ex nor I realized the practicalities of the method and location of exchanges until we experienced it for ourselves. It was the first custody adjustment we made, and we have both been happier with the new changes.

12

KINDERGARTEN BASICS

Mediation and Dispute Resolution Tactics

Solving problems that arise during arguments is a basic skill taught to us as early as kindergarten. Kindergarten throwback rules I like to use when arguing with my ex are:

"Treat others how you would like to be treated."
"Use inside voices."
"Wait your turn to talk, and don't interrupt."
"Keep your hands and feet to yourself."
"When someone misbehaves, they get a time out."
"Listen while others are talking."
"No name-calling or bullying."
"Say 'Please' and 'Thank You.'"

When talking with my ex, I use the skills I learned in kindergarten and my mediation training to reduce conflict.

The most important thing I learned which I use when arguing with my frenemy is to control my tone of voice.

My dad's family is Greek. We are loud. On any given holiday, we can be found fighting to talk. The only thing that gives us a chance to get a word in is when another family member shoves food in their mouth, and like lightning, you have to strike at the opportunity to be heard. My frenemy is from an even bigger, louder family. The need to raise our voices to be heard was ingrained in us as children. So, I have to check my volume button when he and I argue. I also remind him to check his.

Another issue we tend to have pop up in our arguments is *gaslighting*. We are both guilty of minimizing the other's feelings and dismissing them as "ridiculous." This falls under the "treat others as you would like to be treated" portion of my kindergarten argument training. Mediation training taught me that feelings cannot be right or wrong, they just are.

To properly maintain any relationship with your frenemy or otherwise, you have to maintain a level of understanding of the other person's point of view. Invalidation of another person's feelings immediately causes them to become defensive and escalates the argument.

Lifelong Frenemies

With my mediation clients and in my personal interactions, I try to validate the other person's feelings by paraphrasing the way they feel and explaining that it was not my intention to make them feel that way—the goal being that the other person feels their point of view is recognized. Failure to recognize another person's point of view is the number one reason for ineffective arguments because once a person believes that their opinion doesn't matter, they stop trying to find a solution to the problem. This is a particularly difficult balancing act for me.

Invalidation of another person's feelings causes them to become defensive and escalates the argument.

As an attorney, I must remove feelings from my arguments to effectively argue the facts and law of a case to win my argument with the judge.

In mediation, the goal is to validate the parents' feelings so that they both leave satisfied with the solution since mediation is based on the parties' agreement.

I switch gears based on the goals set by my clients.

In my personal life, I have rarely found that arguing the facts and "making my case" goes over well in my personal relationships.

This includes my relationship with my frenemy.

A typical conversation with my frenemy might look something like this:

> **Me:** "I'm having trouble figuring out how to bring the kids to school on Monday and get to my meeting on time. Can you drive them?"
>
> **Him:** "I drove them yesterday, and I have plans to meet a colleague for coffee."
>
> **Me:** "They are your kids too, and my meeting is mandatory. Your coffee is not."
>
> **Him:** "I feel like you don't think anything I do is as important as what you do."
>
> **Me:** Option A: "No, I really don't think it is…it's just coffee."
>
> ***Option B:*** *"I understand that you think I am minimizing your appointment, and I am not trying to, but if I don't attend this meeting on time, it will be a catastrophe. Can you please move your coffee appointment back a half hour? It would mean a lot to me."*

Option B wins, every time. Option B shows the other person that not only do I recognize their feelings and am validating their argument, but I am asking for a favor. Most people like to be in the position to do a favor for another person, so they are willing to accommodate if they are able and asked politely.

While Option A is a true and incidentally hilarious response, it will not attain the desired result, which is my ex actually driving the kids to school. Although Option A is a true statement and it is not by itself insulting, it validates his feeling that I believe my meeting is more important than his plans. **The goal is to achieve the desired result, not to be right.**

You can be right all day, but you still have no way to be two places at once, and the problem still exists. Always say "thank you." Thank you allows the other parent to feel appreciated and will result in better relations and foster better co-parenting. I recognize that my ex did not have to help me that day, but he did. So, I took him to lunch to say thank you. *When amicability fails, try mediation and other custody experts.*

In many cases, the communication breakdown between co-parents is too great to work out. Parents who still prefer to keep custody issues out of court can seek the help of a mediator in solving their disputes. In addition to being a lawyer, I am a Child Custody and Visitation Mediator. Most of the mediation clients I see are required to mediate their dispute under the order of a judge. However, I have mediated custody disputes among parents who prefer not to litigate their disputes in an attempt to maintain amicable relations. Mediators act as a neutral third-party, a referee of sorts, who help the parents communicate their goals and solve their problems without having to go to court.

Most of the time, mediators are attorneys, but sometimes they are mental health professionals or social workers who have additional training in mediation. These professionals can sometimes find solutions to the problems that the parents are too involved in to see objectively. Mediators can also assist with communication between the parents when one parent's voice is stronger than the other's.

I like to think of mediation like solving a puzzle. I look at work schedules to determine the best plan for visitation times.

In most cases, I am able to clearly see a solution to the issues brought to mediation. The parents are not obligated to agree to the solutions I propose, even in court ordered mediation. If at any time either party disagrees with the path that mediation is taking, they can choose to go to the judge with their issues, or if the mediation is voluntary, end the session.

The unique feature of mediation is that the communications that occur between the parents remain confidential.

For parents who typically agree and are having a dispute that they can't move beyond, mediation is an excellent tool to resolve co-parenting problems. In more complicated disputes, such as a parent relocating out of the state, the help of an attorney may be necessary. I recommend mediation for co-parents when issues such as a change of the children's school or a parent's work schedule are the source of the problem.

Mediation is an appropriate tool for minor issues that are creating an inability to compromise.

At the end of mediation, the agreement can be turned into a judgment, in most cases, without the parents ever having to appear in court or incur the high cost and stress that comes with litigation.

Further, mediation can be used for co-parents who are simply having communication issues but otherwise would not change their formal custody arrangement. I have mediated issues that relate to co-parenting planning as opposed to issues that would be found in formal custody judgments. Issues as simple as bedtimes, shared household routines and college savings can be addressed through mediation even though the courts are unlikely to hear those matters in a courtroom setting.

About the Author

Jacqueline Epstein is a child custody mediator and family law attorney in New Orleans, Louisiana. She is the mother of two young daughters, Avivah and Sephorah, with her lifelong frenemy, co-parent and fellow family law attorney, Jeremy Epstein. Jacqueline has served as the chair of the Family Law Committee and as the Liaison to the Commission on Women in the Legal Profession for the American Bar Association Young Lawyer's Division and was a member of the Louisiana State Bar Association Leadership Class. She is currently serving as a member of the Program Planning Committee of the American Bar Association. Since graduating from Georgetown University Law School, where she was internationally published on the topic of comparative family law, she founded Epstein Law Firm, which concentrates its practice on family law. Ms.

Epstein has been named as a Top Lawyer in Family Law by New Orleans Magazine and a Rising Star by Super Lawyers. When she is not mediating disputes on behalf of her clients, her children and herself, she enjoys traveling, cooking and spending time with her daughters.

Appendix

Resources for Education and Extracurricular Activities: Resources for Online Learning, Books, Podcasts and Foreign Language Learning

Library of Congress, http://www.loc.gov

International Children's Digital Library, http://en.childrenslibrary.org

Open Library online, www.openlibrary.org

Wiley Online Library, www.onlinelibrary.wiley.com

Early Learning Resources at the U.S. Department of Education, https://www.ed.gov/early-learning/resources

Free Online College and Pre-college Courses:

Georgetown University, https://www.edx.org/school/georgetownx

Yale University, www.openmedia.yale.edu

University of Massachusetts- Boston, www.ocw.umb.edu

Stanford University, www.itunes.stanford.edu

Columbia University, https://youtube.com/channel/UChzhFUxUZFAQSJZ_Tp4B1fA

Harvard University, https://youtube.com/user/Harvard

Massachusetts Institute of Technology, www.owc.mit.edu

Berklee College of Music, www.berkleeshares.com

The Julliard School- www.open.julliard.edu

Resources for Free and Low Cost Extracurricular Activities:

YMCA, Youth Development Programming, www.ymca.net/youth-development

America's State Parks, www.stateparks.org

National Park Service, www.nps.gov/kids/index.cfm

New Orleans Recreation Department, www.nordc.org/activities/youth-programs/

Houston Parks and Recreation Department, www.houstontx.gov/parks/youthprograms

New York City Recreation Department, www.nycgovparks.org

Chicago Park District, https://apm.activecommunities.com/chicago

City of Atlanta Parks and Recreation, Centers of Hope Afterschool Recreational Program, https://www.atlantaga.gov/government/department/parks-recreation/officeof-recreation/afterschool-program

Washington DC Department of Parks and Recreation, https://dpr.dc.gov/service/kids-camps-co-op

City of Los Angeles Department of Recreation and Parks, www.laparks.org/youth-activities

City of Detroit Recreation Centers, www.detroitmi.gov/Detroit-Opportunities/Programs-for-Youth/faqid/1618

Las Vegas, Clark County Parks and Recreation, www.clarkcountynv.gov/parks/Services/Pages/youth-programs.aspx

City of Miami Parks and Recreation, www.miamigov.com/parks/youthPrograms

Resources for Children with Special Needs:

Easter Seals, www.easterseals.org

Autism Society of America, www.autism-society.org

Do2Learn, www.do2learn.com

Resources for Co-Parenting:

Our Family Wizard, www.ourfamilywizard.org

Brown Bear Family Calendar, www.brownbearsw.com

Lotsa Helping Hands, www.lotsahelpinghands.com

The Center for Parenting Education, www.centerforparentingeducation.org/resource-directory

Share Kids, www.sharekids.com

References

St. Philip v. Montalbano, 108 So. 3d 277 - 2013 - La: Court of Appeals, 4th Cir. 2013. N.d. Print.

J. Kenkade
PUBLISHING®

Ready to Get Published?

Our All-Inclusive Publishing Package

Professional Proofreading & Editing
Interior Design & Cover Design
Manuscript Writing Assistance
Affordable Pricing & More

For Manuscript Submission or other inquiries:
www.jkenkade.com
(501) 482-JKEN

Also Available from J. Kenkade Publishing

I Was the Sitter for My Husband's Wife

An engaging story about a single woman living far away from her family. Rebekah finds herself needing more fulfillment in her life as a nurse. She has been praying to God for her need until one day, He finally answers in the form of two strangers who aren't really strangers at all.

Available for purchase at www.jkenkade.com
Paperback: 978-1-944486-17-4

Also Available from J. Kenkade Publishing

The Art of Living

A dose of inspiration for every day of your life. Each day, we are faced with challenges that we must conquer and overcome. The contents of this book will help you maintain, stay afloat, and solve some of your troubles. There is a skill, a strategy, and an art to living a prosperous and peaceful life.

Available for purchase at www.jkenkade.com
Paperback 978-1-944486-04-4

Also Available from J. Kenkade Publishing

PAYD Thoughts

A collection of poems that focuses on various subjects inspired by the author's experiences shared with the hope of encouraging and inspiring readers in similar situations. "PAYD Thoughts" discusses social issues, love towards God, unhealthy relationships, depression, and more.

Available for purchase at www.jkenkade.com
Paperback 978-1-944486-18-1

www.ingramcontent.com/pod-product-compliance
Lightning Source LLC
Chambersburg PA
CBHW022111090426
42743CB00008B/806